Knitting Patterns For Beginners

A Knitting Patterns Step-by-Step Guide For Beginners With 25 Different Beautiful & Interesting Knitting Patterns Included

Nancy Gordon

Contents

Introduction

So are you interested in creating your own knitting projects? Are you looking for a bit more practice to use to get some cool new projects designed? Do you want to try to create something new without being so stressed out? If so, you're in the right spot. Learning to knit isn't difficult—but you can make it happen if you know what you are doing. All you will have to do is make sure that you can follow a knitting pattern!

Now, this book is a pattern guide. It assumes that you already know the basics of how to knit and assumes that if you are here, you are probably here looking for new patterns to create. This means that we won't be going over basic tutorials of how to start a project or how to begin knitting here. We will be taking a look at all sorts of different ways that you will be able to do the projects that you want to do, and we will dive right in, assuming that you already know. If you don't know, then consider heading over to a beginner's guide instead.

So, are you ready? Let's get practicing to create all those projects that you really want to enjoy!

Chapter 1:

20 Beginners Patterns

Are you ready to get started? These simple beginner patterns are designed to allow you to make your very own projects without too much struggle. As you go through these projects, you will be working to create these projects that look great, are sometimes functional, and are so much fun to make yourself! You can give these as gifts, make them for yourself, or otherwise work to create with them. All you have to do is commit to making your projects the way that you want to, and before you know it, you should be able to find yourself really enjoying the process.

Socks and Scarves and Other Wearables

Easy Baby Booties

Supplies:

- Medium-weight yarn (80 yds)
- Size 8 straight needles

Gauge: 26 S x 32 R

Size: 4 inches

Who doesn't love baby booties? And, even better, who doesn't like making them? They make a great thoughtful gift, too, and you can personalize them to exactly what the other person would want. You can make sure that you get the right colors and size, and you can make a baby keepsake that will last forever. It may be a cherished possession that the new mom has for years to come. And, these are so easy to make that you can have them done in a 30 minute period of time!

To do this project, you will be making two ¾ inch long footbeds that are then wrapped around by two straps of knitted yarn.

Instructions:

1. Create 26 stitches. Then, work in 10 rows of garter stitches.

2. Bind the 10 stitches at the beginning of that next row, then finish it.

3. Bind off 10 stitches at the beginning of your new row. You should have 6 stitches in the middle. Off of that 6 stitches in the middle, use the garter stitch for an additional 20 rows. Then, bind off.

4. You now have a T shape that you will use to wrap into the booties. The top part of the T shape is the back and side of your bootie, while the long, narrow part is the footbed.

5. Take one side of your back and place it on top of the footbed. Then, take the other side of the back and pull it over the other way. They are now crossing over each other into a cute bootie shape. Then, sew the bootie together with a yarn needle, following along the toes and sides. When done, turn the booties inside out to finish.

6. Repeat the process a second time to create two booties.

Supplies:

- Yarn (1 skein)

- Size 7 needles

Gauge: 4 sts = 1 inch

Size: newborn

If you have given away those baby booties, you might want to consider making a baby hat too. This hat can be made with matching yarn for a cute outfit to give to your best friend for her baby shower or for your very own child or grandchild. Do you want to be able to knit your own baby hat? Then follow these steps—before you know it, you'll have it done! To knit here, you will need whatever type of yarn you want, plus your 4mm needles.

Instructions:

1. Start with casting on 60 loops to create the base of your newborn hat.

2. Hold your needles to allow your left needle to hold the knitting on it. The points should be away from you, and the yarn should be coming off of the needle from the right, bottom part of the needle.

3. Start knitting a 5-inch long piece using basic knitting stitches. This will probably be around 50 rows or so. To do this, you will hold the needle with the cast-on loops on your left, with the needle in your right hand passing through the stitch that is behind the left needle. All of your stitches should add one lop to the needle on the right while removing one from the left. When you finish the row, you can switch needles, so you start with the knitting always on the left needle.

4. After about five inches of knitting, start decreasing the length of your rows. Instead of going through one stitch with the right needle, start going through two. Continue to taper in this manner, going by twos until you only have a single loop left on your needle.

5. Cut off the excess yarn while still leaving yourself with a long piece of yarn that you can use to sew the sides of your hat together. Tie a simple knot where it leaves the knitting, then wrap your hat around and start sewing it shut.

6. Once the sides of the hat are sewn together, tie off the end and trim the tail off.

7. Turn the hat inside out. You should now have the stitched seam on the inside. Enjoy!

Supplies:

- Yarn (1 skein)

- 4.5 mm needles

- 1 button

Gauge: 34 sts x 52 r

Size: one size fits most babies

If you have gone this far with creating a pair of booties and a newborn baby hat, you may as well add in a quickly created baby bib as well. This process is so incredibly simple, and to create it, all you will need to do is pay attention to your stitching. This is as simple as creating several rows of knitting and then attaching a buttonhole and button to it to allow yourself to secure the bib to the baby that will be wearing it. Before you know it, you'll have a cute pattern that is perfect for any baby to wear, and if it matches along with the hat and booties, you may even see it featured in some adorable baby photos posted on social media by the lucky parents-to-be!

Instructions:

1. Star cast on 34 stitches. Then, knit every single row with garter stitches until you have a 7-inch long square. This is the perfect foundation for your project.

2. From there, start knitting 10, cast off for 14 stitches, then knit 10 more. This creates the base for your straps that will wrap around the neck of the baby.

3. Working with just one strap at a time, garter stitch the first half of your neckband until it is 5 inches long. Then, for the next row, knit 2 together for 6 rows, tapering the end. For the last row, cast off 9 stitches.

4. Attach some more yarn and begin garter stitching on the second sid3e with garter

stitches. Create 5 inches. Then, knit 3, knit 2 together, pass the yarn over, then knit 2 together, knit 3.

5. Your next row should be knit 9

6. For the last row, cast off 9 stitches. Darn the loose ends and sew on your button.

7. Enjoy your new bib!

Supplies:

- Yarn (4 skeins in varying colors, chunky)
- Size 13 needle

Gauge: 2.5 stitches per inch

Size: Adult

After completing those projects for babies, let's consider some fun projects that you can make for adults as well. At this point, we're looking at ways that you can touch up anyone's outfit with ease. Consider making a nice color block scarf that you can use. In the picture above, you see that this project is making use of red and green, creating a festive Christmas motif, but if you want to, you can make any color that you want. You can choose to use just the two rows, or you could also start making several different colors and having a rainbow scarf. No matter the colors that you choose, however, you can create a nice project that is great for you to keep to yourself, or you could also choose to create one to give as a gift as well! This project is so versatile, and especially if you live somewhere cold, you probably will need to have some sort of scarf pattern that will help you to figure out what you are doing. At the end of the day, you have complete control here. Just figure out what colors you want, figure out how large you want to create your blocks of color, and complete the project! Before long, you'll have a great scarf that you can enjoy!

Keep in mind that this pattern will use the seed or moss stitch to create a nice textured pattern. It will be flat and look the same on both sides, making it perfect for something like a scarf.

Instructions:

1. Cast on 35. Then, for row 1, knit 1 purl 1 until you get to the end.

2. Repeat this process to create a nice block of red for about 2-4 inches (to your personal preference).

3. Change to a second color (green in the picture). At this row, repeat the pattern until you have a nice 8-inch block of green.

4. Change the color back to red. Repeat for another 8-inch block of red.

5. Continue to repeat the process of alternating between red and green for 8-inch segments along your scarf until you have a scarf that is roughly 2 yards long. Cast off, then give your scarf to someone, or enjoy it for yourself!

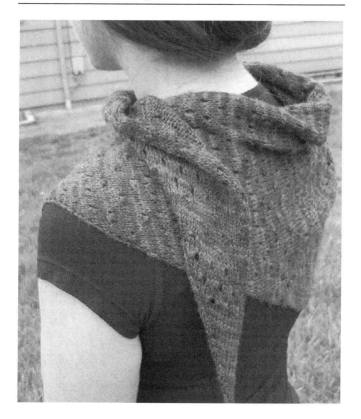

Supplies:

- 480 yards of yarn

- Stitch marker

- Tapestry needle

- US Size 8 circular 40" needle

Gauge: 4 stitches per inch

Size: Adult

If you are looking for a simple project to practice your knitting skills with, try this shawl on for size. Try having fun with this project by trying different yarn color patterns. You can make a shawl for every occasion or make shawls for your friends and family.

Instructions:

1. Make a loop for a slip knot. Run it through the sewing needle with the tail in front. Make it tight. You are going to cast three stitches on it now. There is already one stitch on the needle in this situation. Consider that slip knot as the first stitch.

2. To cast the two following stitches, make use of the long tail technique.

   a. Take the need and go in-between the tail and the yarn ball, and then make the rest of the stitches.

   b. Have your thumb rest on the tail and a finger on the yarn of the yarn ball. Holding this thread, holding the stitch to stabilize it. Turn your finger and thumb back. Go in under your thumb, then go over your finger.

c. Finish by going back through the hole where your thumb was, and your second stitch is done.Lean them around over your finger under your palm, back into your thumb, and tighten. And your three stitches are there.

3. Treat the circular needle just like a straight one and knit your first row that way.

   a. At the start of this row, the pattern increases, and then you just knit straight through the next row. In this first stitch, begin the increase.

   b. Put the right needle behind the left needle and knit the stitch and slip it off the needle instead of sliding it off the needle.

   c. Now that an increase has been made, you should see a purl bump. Then you just need to knit the remaining stitches in a row. Continue knitting row after row, adding an increase at the beginning of each one.

4. Once the shawl reaches your desired size, it is time to start binding off.

5. Knit the first stitch followed by a second stitch.

a. Take the first stitch over the second stitch. Then repeat across the final row. Be mindful not to knit this step too tightly, as the average length of that side of the shawl is going to be tight, and it is going to look awkward.What some people do if they have a problem casting out too tight is turn to another needle. It could be one or two sizes bigger, so they do not have this problem. So, if you feel like you are tight, you should try this and see if you can manage better.

6. If you do not want to use the above option, try to give a little extra slack, and do not pull up for every stitch.

7. To knit the last stitch, pull the yarn end and run it through the final loop.

8. You are going to weave in the ends of the thread. Here is where you will use the tapestry needle to finish the shawl.

9. Weave the needle in a garter pattern. Follow the purl bumps lines.

a. You do it for maybe 4 to 6 stitches, depending on how much thread you have left. The intention is to make it so entrenched that this thread is not going to come loose and unravel. Go

back through a couple of stitches if
you need to.

b. Then, go back in the opposite
    direction a few stitches and follow,
    and that is it. Cut the thread very
    close to the end of the job, being
    careful not to cut the work.

And there you go, a nice shawl to wear out
that you made yourself. Great!

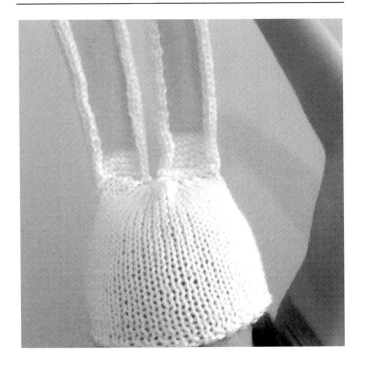

Supplies:

- Bulky white yarn (56 yd)

- bulky pink yarn (7 yd)

- 4 size 10.5 double-pointed needles.

Gauge: 14 stitches and 18 rounds per 4 inches

Size: Baby

Do you have kids that love to play pretend? Need a hat that is perfect for an Easter celebration? Have some other reason that you need an eared hat? No matter why you can make your very own knit bunny ear hat and all you'll have to do is follow some round patterns with bulky yarn. It will be warm enough for those crisp spring mornings hunting for eggs or for some silly fun.

This project will use a simple Stockinette hat pattern. Then, at the top, you will have your stitches picked up so you can create your ears, and then you can knit and stitch the inner part as well. It's quite simple, and yet the results are so incredibly pleasing to the eye! This can be a great gift for the kiddos in your life, or you could probably even sell them if you took the time to practice. All you have to do is get started!

Instructions:

1. Cast on 48 stitches. Divide onto 3 needles, then join in the round.

   a. Work with the knit 2 purl 2 pattern to create ribbing for an inch.

2. Then, change up to the stockinette stitch to go another 2 inches.

a. Knit 6, knit 2 together. Repeat.

b. Knit 1 round.

c. Knit 5, knit 2 together. Repeat again.

d. Knit 1 round.

e. Knit 4, knit 2 together. Repeat again.

f. Knit 3, knit 2 together. Repeat again.

g. Knit 2, knit 2 together. Repeat again.

h. Knit 1 round.

i. Knit 2 together. Then repeat again.

3. Cut your yarn while still leaving behind a nice, long tail.

   a. Thread the yarn onto your yarn needle. Then, slip your stitches onto yarn and pull tightly.

4. Then, start knitting the ears. Choose somewhere on the top where ears would naturally fall, then work down. Knit 9 stitches.

   a. Again, you will be doing the stockinette stitch for 8 inches.

   b. Then, knit 4, knit 2 together.

   c. Knit 1 row.

d. Stockinette knit, knit 2, knit 2 together.

e. Knit 1 row.

f. Stockinette knit, knit 2 together.

g. Knit 1 row.

h. Knit 2 together to finish. Trim yarn.

i. Repeat 15-23 on the other ear.

5. Then, take your contrast yarn (the pink of the inner ear). Cast on 9 stitches. Then, work to create the inner ear. Sew the pink lining into the ear, then put the right sides out.

Supplies:

- Worsted yarn (8 yards)
- Size 8 needles
- Darning needles
- Buttons
- Sewing needles for buttons

Gauge: 36 stitches and 16 rows

Size: 1 size fits all

Does the current pandemic have you wishing that you could wear a mask without your ears feeling like they're about to fall off? No one really enjoys having to wear masks, and with how uncomfortable they all are, who can blame us? We don't like those feelings of elastic, and while you can get masks with ties, you have to worry about the ties becoming undone as well or having your kids pull them off. There has to be a better solution, right?

Well, you're in luck because there is an incredibly simple solution to these problems, and you can solve them just by knowing how to work your way around the knitting needles! All you have to do is choose to get started, and before you know it, you'll have the result you wanted! Instead of having those uncomfortable ear loops resting against your ears, you can knit your very own ear savers! These are just little straps of knitted material that will rest against the back of your head to allow you to simply drape your mask straps to the buttons on them. Then, the tension is there, you get a tighter fit, and you can avoid running into all sorts of those common problems that are going to cause you discomfort. And, all you have to do is knit a bit to get everything right where you want it. Before you know it, your pattern is complete!

Even better, these only take a short amount of time to make, and you can then add your buttons to make them entirely adjustable. This means that being able to put these on should be incredibly easy and allow you plenty of time to do them your way!

Instructions:

1. To start, cast on 4 stitches. You now have 4 stitches on your needle.

2. For row 1, on the back of the project, knit 4.

3. For row 2, slip around. Then, slip stitch 1, knit 1 through the front and back loop (increasing the pattern one loop). Knit 1 through the front and back loop. Purl 1.

4. For row 3, on the Wrong Side, slip stitch 1, knit 1 through the front and the back loop. Knit 2, knit 1 through the front and back loop. Purl 1.

5. For row 4, on the front side, slip stitch 1. Then, knit until one stitch is left. Then purl 1.

    a. Repeat row 4 until you have a piece that is between 4.75 and 5.75 inches long, depending on the length that you want. Then end on a row that is facing the right way up.

6. To finish, for row 5 on the back, slip stitch 1, knit 2 together, knit 2, slip slip knit, purl 1.

7. For row 6, on the right side, slip stitch 1, knit 2 together, slip slip knit, purl 1.

8. Bind your cord and weave into the ends.

   a. Sew up two buttons into place on either end of the strap. Then, enjoy! These are an easy way to protect your ears.

This pattern can be adjusted, as well. If you want it for children, you could make it smaller or put the buttons closer to the center as well to make it a tighter, slimmer fit.

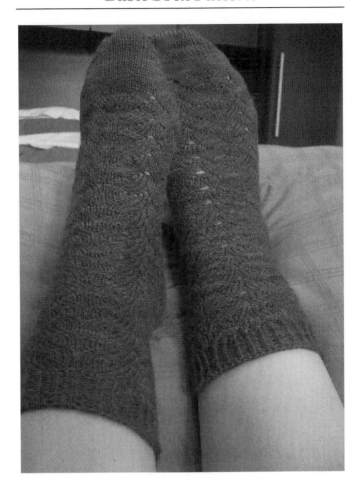

Supplies:

- US Size 1 needles (4 to 5 pairs of double-pointed needles)

- Yarn Needle or Crochet hook

- Stitch holder

- 1 skein (for women's sizes) or 2 skeins (for men's sizes) of yarn/465 yards

Gauge: 32 sts, 48 r

Size: Adult

Instructions:

1. To make the leg, use the US 1 needles to cast on 68 using the long tail method. Arrange the stitches as evenly as you can on 3 double-pointed needles. Place the stitch holder and join. Do not twist the stitches.

   a. Knit 2, purl 2, ribbing until your piece measures 3 inches (7.5 cm). Keep working using a stocking stitch until your piece measures 8 inches (20.5 cm) or your desired length.

   b. To make the heel, knit across 17 stitches. Turn your work and purl across 34 stitches.

   c. Place 34 instep stitches on a spare needle or stitch holder and work them later.

2. Using the eye or partridge stitch pattern, begin the heel flap. Work back and forth on the heel stitches like this:

- Row one: Slip one purlwise with yarn in back. Knit one and continue to end.

- Row two: Slip one purlwise with the yarn on the front. Purl to end.

3. Repeat rows 1 and 2 until you have 34 rows. You should have 17 chain selvage stitches on both edges of the project.

4. For the turn, heal do the following:

- Row 1: Knit across 19 stitches, slip-slip-knit, knot 1. Turn the project over.

- Row 2: Slip 1 purlwise, purl 5, purl 2 together, purl 1, turn.

- Row 3: Slip 1 purlwise, knit 1 stitch before gap, slip-slip-knit with a stitch on each side of the gap, knit 1, turn.

- Row 4: Slip 1 purlwise, purl to 1 stitch before gap, purl 2 together (with 1 stitch from each side of gap), purl 1, turn.

a. Repeat rows 3 and 4 until all the heel stitches are worked. End in a row 4.

5. For the Heel gusset, knit across all heel stitches, and with double-pointed needles (needle 1), knit 17 stitches along the selvage edge of the heel flap.

    a. With double-pointed needles (needle 2), work them across the instep stitches from earlier.

    b. With more double-pointed needles (needle 3), knit 17 stitches along the other side of the heel and knit across half of your heel stitches. You should have a total of 88 stitches.

6. For the center back heel, round 1 will be:

    a. use needle 1 to knit to the last three stitches on needle 1.

    b. Knit 2 together, knit 1.

    c. Knit across all the instep stitches on needle 2.

    d. Starting at the beginning of needle 3, knit 1, slip slip knit, and knit to the end. Two gusset stitches should be decreased.

    e. For round 2, knit.

    f. Repeat rounds 1 and 2 until you have 68 stitches.

7. For the foot, work using a stocking stitch pattern until your project measures 6.5 inches in length.

8. For the toe, do the following for round 1:

    a. Needle 1 knit to the last three stitches, knit 2 together, knit 1.

    b. For needle 2, knit 1, slip slip knit, knit to the last 3 stitches, then knit 2 together, knit.

    c. For needle 3, knit 1, slip-slip-knit, knit to the end. For round 2, knit.

    d. Repeat rounds 1 and 2 until you have 32 stitches. From there, only repeat round 1 until only 12 stitches remain.

9. Knit the stitches from needle 1 onto needle 2. You should have 6 stitches on both needles.

    a. Cut your yarn, leaving an 18-inch tail. Knit the two sides of the toe together and sew the loose ends. You are done!

Toys and Other Fun Projects

Knitted Cat Toys

Supplies:

- 3.5 mm needles
- 15 g color A yarn
- 15 g color B yarn
- 5 g accent color yarn (ears, nose, tail)
- Stuffing

Gauge: Gauge is irrelevant as this is not for wearing

Size: Irrelevant as this is not for wearing. Estimated to be about 4 inches long

Cats and yarn go together almost as well as cats and mice... So why not put all three together? With this pattern, you are going to make your very own knitted cat toys that you can toss around for your cat to drive them wild! If you want to, you can stuff 'em up with catnip to add that extra appeal, too. But, these little mouse patterns are certain to please just about any furry friend. Enjoy these patterns and find out just why so many people love to make their very own cat toys!

Creating this project is simple, too, so long as you have got plenty of yarn, knitting needles, stuffing to fill it up with, a squeaker if you want it to make some sounds, a pouch to hold catnip, and the determination to do the project. From the tip of the nose to the end of the tail, this project is roughly 4 inches long, making it the perfect size for your feline friend. This project works with two colors to make a nice stripe pattern that's extra fun for your cat to chase around.

Instructions:

1. Start by casting two stitches in your first color. Then, complete the pattern as followed:

   a. For row 1, knit all the way across.

   b. For row 2, purl all the way across.

   c. For row 3, knit 1, make one stitch, knit (you have 3 stitches now)

   d. For row 4, purl all the way across.

   e. For row 5, knit 1, make one stitch, knit 1, make one stitch, knit (you have 5 stitches now).

   f. For row 6, purl all the way across.

   g. For row 7, knit 1, make one stitch, knit 3, make 1 stitch, knit 1 (you have 7 stitches now).

   h. For row 8, Purl across.

   i. For row 9, knit 1, make 1 stitch, knit 5, make 1 stitch, knit 1 (you have 9 stitches now.)

   j. For row 10, purl across.

   k. For row 11, knit 1, make one stitch, knit 7, make one stitch, knit 1 (you have 11 stitches now.)

l. For row 12, purl across.

m. For row 13, knit 1, make one stitch, knit 9, make 1 stitch, knit 1. You have 13 stitches now).

n. For row 14, purl across.

o. For row 15, knit 1, make 1 across, knit 11, make 1 stitch, knit 1 (you have 15 stitches now).

p. For row 16, purl across.

q. For row 17, knit 1, make 1 stitch, knit 13, make 1 stitch, knit 1 (you have 17 stitches).

r. For row 18, purl across.

2. Change to your second color.

   a. For row 19, knit 1, make 1 stitch, knit 15, make 1 stitch, knit 1 (you have 19 stitches).

   b. For row 20, purl across.

3. Change back to your first color.

   a. For row 21, knit 1, make 1 stitch, knit 17, make 1 stitch, knit 1 (you have 21 stitches).

   b. For row 22, purl across.

4. Change back to color 2.

a. For row 23, knit 1, make 1 stitch. Knit 19, make 1 stitch. Knit 1 (you have 23 stitches.)

b. For row 24, purl across.

5. Change back to color 1.

a. For row 25, knit 1, make 1 stitch, knit 21, make 1 stitch, knit 1 (you have 25 stitches).

b. For row 26, purl across.

6. Change to color 2.

a. For row 27, knit across.

b. For row 28, purl across.

7. Change back to color 1.

a. For rows 29-35, repeat steps for rows 27 and 28, alternating colors every two rows. Your last row should be knit in the first color.

b. For row 36, purl across in the first color.

8. Cut off roughly 7 inches of yarn.

a. Thread the yarn through the leftover stitches, then draw tight to make a tail end of the mouse that is round.

9. Then, create the ears.

a. Cast on 5 stitches in pink.

b. For row 1, knit across.

c. For row 2, purl across.

d. For row 3, knit all the way across

e. For row 4, purl across.

f. For row 5, knit across.

g. Cut off 10cm of yarn.

h. Use the yarn to thread through stitches to draw tight and make a rounded ear. Darn the end.

i. Sew the cast on yarn through the bottom stitches and pull tightly to make the lower part of your ear.

10. To finish the project, sew both sides of the mouse body together from tail to nose, lining up the stripes as you go. Leave a hole to fill with stuffing.

a. Push in stuffing and squeaker and catnip into the body.

b. Sew the body all the way to the tip of the nose.

c. Attach your ears with sewing.

d. Embroider the nose with a pink dot of yarn, running the end of the yarn through the body and out the tail.

e. Tie a knot at the end of your tail.

f. Add eyes with embroidery.

g. Give it a good look over, then throw it to the cat to enjoy!

Supplies:

- Size 7 double-pointed needles
- Stitch markers
- Stitch holders
- Worsted yarn (170 yds)
- Scrap yarn (few small pieces)
- Crochet hook

Gauge: 16 sts = roughly 4 inches

Size: 1 large

Want to make your very own little hand puppet that you can use? Maybe you're still making those gifts for people. Maybe you want to make a puppet for your own kids or someone else's. Either way, these can be fun projects to make if you know some children in need of finding their very own patterns that they can enjoy and play with as well. All you will need to do is make sure that you follow these instructions, and before you know it, you'll have your own puppets that you can enjoy. This puppet will be a cute little puppet base. If you want to change the animal that it is, all you would need to do is change up the ears and accessories that you add. In this particular tutorial, we'll be making a cute little mouse.

Instructions:

1. With double-pointed needles, cast on 36 stockinette stitches. You will have 12 on each of your three needles. Join them without twisting, then mark the beginning of your round.

    a. For round 1-5, knit 2, purl 2, then repeat for all 5 rounds.

2. Change to the stockinette knit stitch and work it until your piece is 6 inches from the cuff.

a. Place 18 stockinettes to hold as your lower jar. Then, divide your remaining 18 stockinettes between 2 needles (with 9 on each). On needle 3, cast on 18 stockinettes for the inside of your mouth.

b. Then, start working on the head. Work 8 rounds in stockinette knit stitch.

c. Begin with needle 1 (the first 9 stockinettes from earlier). Knit 1, slip slip knit, knit to the end of the needle.

d. On needle 2, knit to the last 3 stockinettes. Knit 2 together, knit 1.

e. On needle 3, knit 1, slip slip knit, knit to last 3 stockinettes, knit 2 together. Knit 1-32.

f. Then, for rounds 2-7 of the head, knit all around.

g. For round 8, work in decreasing rounds for 28 stockinettes.

h. Knit around for rounds 9-12.

i. For round 13, work decreasing rounds for 24 stockinettes.

j. For 14 and 15, knit around.

k. For 16, work decreasing rounds—you have 20 stockinettes.

l. Round 17, knit all around.

m. Repeat decreasing rounds every round until you have just 8 stockinettes. Cut the yarn, then pull the end through all stockinettes twice before securing.

3. Then, create a lower mouth. Divide the stockinettes from the holder between 2 needles (9 on each). On the third needle, pick up and knit 18 stockinettes across. Cast-on stockinettes inside the mouth. Work 6 rounds in stockinette knit stitch.

a. Round 1, work in decreasing rounds for 32 stitches.

b. For 2-5, knit around.

c. For round 6, work decreasing rounds to 28 stitches.

d. For rounds 7 and 8, knit around.

e. For round 9, work decreasing rounds for 24 stitches

f. Round 10, knit around. Repeat decreasing rounds until you have just 4 remaining. Fasten it off. This is what you see in the picture above, though in the picture, multiple colors were used.

4. From there, you can start making anything else that you want out of your puppet. In the photo, there were buttons added as eyes and a nose. If you want to make a pig or a cat, you will change up the ears and eyes to match. For us, we are going to continue on with our mouse puppet.

    a. Take your base puppet to the beginning of the head.

    b. Knit rounds 1-8 around. For round 9, work decreasing rounds.

    c. For rounds 10-15, knit around.

    d. Round 16, work decreasing rounds to 28 stitches.

    e. For rounds 17-20, knit around.

    f. For round 21, work decreasing rounds to 24.

    g. Rounds 22 and 23, knit around.

    h. For round 24, work descending rounds to 20.

    i. For round 25, knit around.

    j. For round 26, work descending rounds to 16.

k. For rounds 27-32, repeat rows 25 and 26 for four sets.

l. Cut all yarn, then pull it through and fasten securely.

5. Make the ears. Cast on 5.

    a. Knit, including 1 stockinette at the beginning of every row. DO this 10 times.

    b. Rows 6-12, knit across.

    c. Rows 13-18, knit 2 together, knit across 4 times.

    d. Then, make your tongue. Cast 5. Then, knit across for rows 1-6.

6. For 7 and 8, knit 2 together, knit across. Then bind off the last 3 stitches.

    a. Assemble your puppet. Sew the ears to the head. Then, sew the tongue into the mouth.

    b. Take black yarn to make the eyes and nose. Enjoy!

Supplies:

- Size 5 needles
- 80 yds yarn

Gauge: Irrelevant as this is not being worn

Size: Rougly 4 inches long

Want to make an adorable hedgehog pattern that is so cute you can't help but want to give it to all of your friends' children? These are adorable patterns that you can make to create your very own hedgehog pattern that just about anyone would love to have on hand. All you have to do is make sure that you work to get the stitching just right.

To do this project, you will need plenty of yarn, scissors, stuffing, and tapestry needles. But, it is such a cute project that is absolutely worth it! The project that you'll have in the end is cuter than any so far, and you can learn a lot from all of the stitching that you will have to do and to create the various pieces that you will be doing. It's quite the project, and you'll be able to see just how satisfying it is to finish when you have your very own fuzzy little guy waiting on the shelves for you. All you'll have to do is have the patience and fortitude to make it!

Ears (Make 2)

1. Cast off 8 stockinette stitches in contrasting color, join in the round
2. Round 1: knit into the front and back of 16 stitches
3. Knit every round till it measures about 1/2 inches, then cast off weave in top end and attach to the hedgehog.

Back of Body:

1. In the main color cast off 4 stockinette stitches

2. Row 1: knit front and back, knit 2 , knit front and back (you now have 6 stitches.)

3. Row 2: purl front and back, purl 4, purl front and back (you now have 8 stitches)

4. Row 3: knit front and back, knit 6, knit front and back(you now have 10 stitches)

5. Row 4: purl front and back, purl 8, purl front and back (you now have 12 stitches)

6. Work in stockinette stitch for about 10 rows 2 inches from cast on, end after a purl row.

7. Decreasing

8. Row 1: slip, slip, knit, knit 8 stitches, knit 2 together (you now have 10 stitches)

9. Row 2: purl 2 together, purl 6 stitches, purl 2 together (you now have 8 stitches)

10. Row 3: slip, slip, knit, knit 4, knit 2 together (you now have 6 stitches)

11. Row 4: purl 2 together, P2, purl 2 together (you now have 4 stitches)

Body:

Continued from the back of the body

1. Knit the 4 stockinette stitches on the needle, on the same needle, pick up 10stockinette stitches around the back of the body, continuing around till there are 42stockinette stitches, 14 per needle

2. Round 1: Knit front and back, knit to the last stockinette stitch on needle, knit through front and back; repeat for each needle: 16 stockinette stitches per needle (48)

   a. Repeat Round 1 again, then 18 stockinette stitches per needle (You now have 54 stitches total)

3. Knit every round alternation between pulled curl stitch and knit around till about 1 1/2 inches long. Try 1 pulled curl stitch round and 2 knit rounds for less work, it doesn't create as full of a look.

   a. Figure out where the belly of your hedgehog is and always knit that needle.

   b. Create a curled stitch; knit into a stockinette stitch, then tug it out 2 inches, twist around your finger, then put it back onto your needle. Knit normal and curled stitch together.

4. Decreasing Rounds continue alternating between normal knit and curled stitches

   a. Round 1: Knit 7, knit 2 together, then repeat 16 stockinette stitches per needle (You now have 48 stitches total)

   b. Rounds 2-5: Knit all (4 rounds total)

   c. Round 6: Knit 6, knit 2 together, then repeat 14 stockinette stitches per needle (you now have 42 stitches total)

   d. Round 7: Knit 5, knit 2 together, then repeat 12 stockinette stitches per needle (you now have 36 stitches total)

   e. Round 8: Knit all

   f. Round 9: Knit 4, knit 2 together, 10 stockinette stitches per needle (you now have 30 stitches total)

   g. Round 10: Knit all (end on the curled round)

   h. Round 11: Switch to contrasting color and stop curl stitches. Knit all

   i. Round 12: Knit 2 together, knit to last 2 stockinette stitches on the needle, knit 2 together, repeat 8 stockinette stitches per needle (you now have 24 stitches total)

j.   Round 13-17: knit all (5 rounds). Begin stuffing as you go

k.   Round 18: Knit 2 together, knit to last 2 stockinette stitches on the needle, knit 2 together, repeat 6 stockinette stitches per needle (you now have 18 stitches total)

l.   Round 19-21: knit all (3 rounds)

m.   Round 22: Knit 2 together, knit to last 2 stockinette stitches on needle, knit 2 together repeat 4 stockinette stitches per needle (you now have 12 stitches total)

n.   Round 23: Knit all

o.   Round 24: Knit 2 together, 2 stockinette stitches per needle (you now have 6 stitches total)

5.   Finish stuffing. Cut the yarn, leaving a long tail. Pull the end through the remaining stockinette stitches, gather up tight to close the hole, and stitch to secure. Weave your leftover yarn to the inside. Trim off the remainder, then attach your nose and eyes.

Housewares, Décor, and More

Maybe you want something a bit more robust or a bit more useful than having a cat toy or a cute bunny hat. For that, you have got all sorts of housewares and other useful tools, such as the ones in this chapter. If you want to have something useful, consider making a coaster, a placemat, or even a pillow. All of these projects in this section are great ways for you to practice without having any issues and without causing you any struggles. Before you know it, you'll have the projects down, and you can start knitting all sorts of different things.

Supplies:

- Size 8 needle

- 1 skein yarn, any size; jut make sure it is a material that will wash well.

Gauge: Irrelevant as this is not for wearing

Size: 5 inches in diameter

We all need coasters sometimes. After all, cold drinks are covered in condensation, and who wants that damaging their table? Most people have a use for coasters if they have any wooden furniture in their entertaining spaces, and because of that, they need a way to make them. So, why not make your own? After all, you can get little paper coasters that are disposable, or you could also choose a nice looking solid coaster that might look great, but they end up dripping everywhere along the way as well. What would be better is finding a nice knitted coaster—one that is absorbent enough to prevent a mess but is also substantial enough to last through the laundry! That's what this project is here for, and they are incredibly simple to make, too. All you have to do is follow the steps that will be provided.

Gather up whatever yarns you want to use. Then, get your needles. Then, it's time to start knitting! For this project, you want a yarn that will felt, knitting needles, a crochet hook for easy access, a bag, a washing machine, and something heavy to flatten your project. When you have everything, you're ready to get started!

1. Cast on 50 stitches, then arrange them on the double pointed needles.

2. Join together into a round, then place a ring marker at the first and last stitches.

   a. For round 1, knit.

   b. For round 2, purl.

   c. For round 3, knit.

   d. For round 4, knit 3, knit 2 together, yarn over, and repeat until you get to the end of the round.

   e. For round 5, knit.

   f. For round 6, knit 3, knit 2 together, then repeat until the end of the round. You now have 40 stitches remaining.

   g. For rounds 7 and 8, knit across.

   h. For round 9, knit 2, then knit 2 together and repeat until the end of the round. You now have 30 stitches remaining.

   i. For rounds 10 and 11, knit all the way around.

j. For round 12, knit 1, knit 2 together, and repeat all the way around. You now have 20 stitches left.

k. For round 13, knit all the way around.

l. For round 14, knit 2 together all the way around. You have 10 stitches remaining.

3. Bind off the last 5 stitches, then weave in the ends. Use a block or a book or something else heavy to flatten them into place gently.

4. Repeat all steps 3 more times to have a set of 4. Enjoy!

Supplies

- Yarn in colors of your choice (green, beige, and brown in the picture above). You can use one color and forego the color changes, or you can alternate more than these three colors if you prefer. We will label the colors A, B, and C. 1 skein of each.

- 4mm knitting needles

- Crochet hook

Gauge: 50sts, 200 r

Size: appx. 12" x 18"

Tables hardly look complete when they aren't set with a nice placemat there to bring the whole thing together. Placemats are not only decorative, helping to bring everything together into something that is quite nice to behold; they are also typically quite nice to have there to pick up any messes. By covering your table up, you can make for easy cleaning in a pinch. If anything spills, you can simply pick up your placemat and toss it into the laundry to clean it, saving yourself from having to scrub the surface of the table or from having your dishes scrape up the finish of the table either.

Instructions:

1. Cast on 50 stitches in color A. Knit 10 rows.

2. Change to color B. Knit 20 rows.

3. Change to color C. Knit 20 rows.

4. Change to color A. Knit 20 rows.

5. Repeat in that order, always knitting 20 rows of each color. End on color A, knitting another 10 rows of A.

6. Cast off. Enjoy!

Supplies:

- 308 yards of 7-gauge yarn

- Pillow foam or other stuffing material

- Size US 17 knitting needles

Gauge: Irrelevant as this is not for wearing.

Size: 24" x 24"

If you are looking for a simple project to make that gives you something comfy to use when you are done, then look no further than this pillow recipe. The following instructions will give you a pillow measuring 24" by 24". Use them as throw pillows for the couch or for a little dash of "you" on your bed.

Instructions:

1. You need to cast a total of 36 stitches. Follow this pattern:

    a. Row 1: Right side, knit.

    b. Row 2: Knit 1, purl 1. Repeat until end of the row.

    c. Repeat this pattern until the length of the project measures 24". End on a wrong-side row. Cast off.

    d. Repeat steps 1 and 2 to get the second side of your pillow.

2. To finish your pillow, sew three sides of the front and back pieces. Insert pillow foam or stuffing, then sew the fourth side closed and enjoy your homemade pillow!

Supplies:

- Size 50 knitting needles

- 4 skeins of yarn in the color of your choice

- Tapestry needle

- Scissors

Gauge: 1 stitch and 1.5 rows/inch

Size: 60" x 80"

Did you think that you'd have to do a lot to be able to make a knit blanket? It's actually easier than you probably thought. This pattern is so simple that you'll be able to get it done relatively simply. You will only need a few simple tools, too!

This pattern is made by holding two strands of yarn together, allowing it to become even bulkier than it would have otherwise been. We'll make this in several different panels that you can then attach together.

Panels 1 and 3

1. Cast off 20 stitches.

2. Row 1: Knit all the way across.

3. Row 2: Purl all the way across.

4. Repeat rows 1 and 2 until the panel is 5 feet long. Bind off and weave in the ends.

Panel 2

1. Cast off 20 stitches.

2. Knit all rows.

3. Continue to knit all rows until the panel is 5 feet long. Bind off all stitches and weave in the ends.

Using your tapestry needle, sew together your three panels, with panel 2 in the middle. Then, weave in all ends to finish.

Supplies:

- Yarn (100% cotton to withstand water), 1 skein

- Knitting needles (size 7)

Gauge: 4.5 sts= 1"

Size: 10" at diagonal point

Need a dishcloth? Who doesn't? Why waste your money buying sponges that can only be used for a short period of time when you could also buy a dishcloth that you can use and reuse again and again? This is a great pattern for beginners to get started on, and it's practical too!

Instructions:

1. Cast on 4.

2. Knit 4.

3. Knit 2, yarn over, knit to the end.

4. Repeat step 3 until you've got 45 stitches across (or more or less, depending upon the size you want.)

5. Knit 1, knit 2 together, yarn over, knit 2 together, knit to end.

6. Repeat step 5 until you have just 4 stitches left.

7. Cast off.

8. Put the end of the yarn through your last loop, tighten it, and hide both ends.

Seasonal Patterns

Sometimes, you want something a bit more seasonal to match up with what you see all around you. For this, you have got all sorts of projects that serve as great seasonal statement pieces just for you! Look at these projects if you want a nice pumpkin for the fall season, a cactus to enjoy in the summer heat, or a knitted snowman to help you feel a bit more festive this winter season. Before you know it, you'll have everything that you need to feel like your home is decorated and enjoyable! So, what are you waiting for? Let's get started!

Supplies:

- Green yarn (1 skein)

- Yarn in the colors for your flower. You will need at least three different colors—the center color, the inner ring color, and the outer petal color. (1 skein each color)

- 4 double-ended knitting needles (2.75mm)

- Crochet hook (2.75 mm)

- Gummed tape

- Scissors

- Tapestry needle

- Toy stuffing

- Wire cutters

Gauge: Irrelevant here as this is not for wearing

Size: 5 inches across

Flowers make a great touch to just about any springtime table, especially bundled up into a nice vase. But, live flowers just don't have the staying power that we wish they did. They will eventually wilt and die, leaving us to pick some more. But, if you want something seasonal that you can use to help yourself decorate, why not consider knitting your very own set of flowers? That's right—you can simply knit a bouquet and have exactly what you wanted.

This particular pattern creates a gerbera daisy—a flower that can come in just about any color out there. No matter the yarn that you have on hand, you'll probably be able to find a daisy with that color scheme. And, even if it doesn't exist in the wild, you can still feel free to make your flowers in any color that you want. We will be going over the template for just one flower here, but if you make several, you can tie them together into a beautiful bouquet to use on your table without worrying about what would happen to the flowers. Have fun and get creative with the colors that you choose!

Instructions:

Creating the petals

1. Take the color that you have chosen for your petals and tie a slip knot. Place the slip knot on your crochet hook.

   a. Then, cast on 11 stitches, using the crochet cast on method.

   b. Knit 8, then bring the yarn to the front of the knitting with one stitch. Slip stitch 1, then turn around the piece.

   c. Bring the yarn to the front of the knitting, then slip stitch 1, purl 7. Turn the piece around.

d. Knit 5, bring the yarn to the front of the knitting, slip stitch 1, then turn the piece around.

e. Bring the yarn to the front of the knitting, then slip stitch 1, purl 6.

f. Cast off 10 stitches.

g. Take the final stitch and transfer it to a crochet hook.

2. Steps 1-8 create just one petal. Repeat 31 more times to get a total of 32 petals.

3. Cut the yarn and thread it through the remaining stitch.

Creating the center

1. Identify your outer color and inner color that you have chosen.

a. Using the outer color, cast on 24 stitches and join into the round.

b. For round 1, knit all stitches to the end of the round.

c. For round 2, knit 2 together through the back of the stitch, knit 1. Repeat 8 times (you have 16 stitches remaining).

d. Change to your inner color.

e. For round 3, purl to the end of the round.

f. For round 4, knit to the end of the round.

g. For round 5, knit 2 together through the back of the loops, then knit 2. Do this 4 times (you have 12 stitches remaining).

h. For round 6, knit 1, knit 2 together through the back of the loops. Repeat 4 times (you have 8 stitches remaining).

2. Thread yarn through remaining stitches and pull tightly.

Creating the stalk

1. Cast on 5 stitches of green and i-cord, between 16 and 20cm.

a. Separate your 5 stitches onto 3 needles.

b. For round 1, knit into front and back 5 times (You have ten stitches)

c. For round 2, knit all the way around.

d. For round 3, knit into front and back, then knit 1. Repeat 5 times (you have 15 stitches)

e. For round 4 and 5, knit all the way around.

Putting it together

1. Take the center of your flower. Reverse, so you are looking at the backside of the center. There are 16 stitches at the color change boundary. Sew one petal to each of those stitches.

2. Then, repeat a second layer of petals atop the first.

3. Cut a piece of wire the length of your stem and cover the end with gummed tape, so it doesn't push out of the knitting. Insert the wire into the stem. Then, attach the cast off end of the stalk to the back of your petals. Put a bit of stuffing into the point where the petals and stalk connect.

4. Sew in any remaining ends that aren't attached. You now have 1 flower. Repeat all steps from start to finish until you've got as many flowers as you want.

Supplies:

- Size 15 16" circular knitting needles

- 1 skein of yarn in your favorite chunky or bulky pumpkin-y color (you'll use less)

- Toy stuffing to bulk up the pumpkin and add support

- Green yarn for the stem

- Scissors

- Tapestry needle

Gauge: Irrelevant as this is not for wearing

Size: 4 inches tall, plus stem

Do you want to prepare for the turning of autumn? Do you love pumpkins and all things Halloween? This pumpkin pattern can help you ensure that you are making your very own decorations, and if you wanted to, you could even slap on some knitted or felted eyes and make a knitted jack-o-lantern instead without much trouble at all. At the end of the day, being able to make your own pumpkin affords you the opportunity to create a beautiful decoration or statement piece on your shelf in your entryway. If you want to enjoy those nice statement pieces, all you have to do is make them yourself! And, this pumpkin is so incredibly simple to make—it won't take you long at all! This chunky pattern works quickly when using large knitting needles, and bulky yarn will help you to make the pattern quickly.

Instructions:

1. Cast on 40 stitches, then join to knit in the round. Keep a marker there, so you know where they joined.

   a. For round 1, knit 2, purl 2, and repeat for the entire round.

   b. For rounds 2 through 24, repeat round 1.

2. Cut the yarn, making sure that you leave a nice, long tail.

   a. Use a tapestry needle to pull the yarn through every stitch on the needle. Then, cinch it closed and tie it off.

   b. On the other end, stuff the pumpkin full of stuffing until you get to the desired thickness.

   c. Then, take another strand of yarn and sew the bottom of the tube shut as well. Push your yarn up through the center of the bottom of the pumpkin and up through the top of it. This will be your anchoring point to secure your pumpkin's stem.

3. Using the color desired for your stem (green in the picture), cast on 6 stitches and secure to work in the round.

   a. For round 1, knit into front and back of the stitch, then knit, and repeat.

   b. For round 2 knit around the entire round.

   c. Repeat step 7 until your stem is the desired length.

   d. Knit 1, knit 2 together and repeat all around.

e. Knit 1, knit 2 together and repeat all
    around.

f. Cut off your yarn, leaving a tail, and
    use the tail and a tapestry needle to
    secure the round, closing it up.

g. Take your tail left on the top of your
    pumpkin and weave it into the
    bottom of the stem. Secure and
    enjoy.

Supplies:

- Yarn (1 skein per color used)

- 3.5mm double-pointed needles

- 3.5mm crochet hook

- Toy stuffing

- Mini flower pots

- Stitch holder

Gauge: Irrelevant as it is not for wearing

Size: Varies

Does summer heat have you down? Do you feel like your kitchen is a desert with how hot it's been? If so, you're in the right spot—don't let your place fail to look the part! Putting up your own cactus in your kitchen can be a lighthearted way to celebrate the summer while enjoying the process of knitting all at the same time. You can enjoy creating these beautiful cactus patterns with ease. You just have to make sure that you take the time to actually create them. By making your own cactus, you can enjoy the look! And even better, these cacti companions are entirely spikey-free! There are no prickly tips here, and that means that you will be able to make them all with ease.

Really, all you have to do is knit in the round, and even though it is a round project, if you find that your stitches aren't perfectly even, you'll still be okay—primarily due to the fact that your cactus can be as knobby as you want it to be without any concern since cacti themselves are quite knobby! This is quite simple to make, and all you have to do is gather up the different items that you'll need and get started!

To complete this project, you will need to follow these steps:

For the small round cactus

1. Cast on 48 stitches with your double-pointed needles. Divide evenly over 4 and put a stitch marker at the beginning of the round, connecting the stitches into a round.

2. Round 1: Knit 1 through the back of the loop, then purl 1. Repeat for the whole round.

3. Repeat round 1 for 30 rounds.

4. Break the yarn off, with a long tail behind. Thread the tail through the darning needle. Pass the needle through all stitches on the double-pointed needles, dropping them off as you do. Pull tightly to close up the hole and fasten, weaving in the loose end ad

stuffing with fiberfill. Sew up the bottom.

For the tall cactus

1. Cast on 30 stitches onto your double-pointed needles. Divide evenly over 4 needles and put a stitch marker at the beginning of the round. Join into a round.

2. For round 1, knit 1 to the back of the loop, purl 1, and repeat to the end of the round.

3. For rounds 2-30, repeat round 1.

4. Join in mohair and keep working with both yarns for an additional 20 rounds.

5. Break off your yarn with a long tail at the end. Thread it through your darning needle. Push the needle through all stitches on your needles, dropping as you go. Pull tightly and fasten. Weave in the loose end, then stuff it up with filling before sewing the bottom. Tease gently to make your cactus look fuzzy.

For the bobbled cactus

1. Start with making the large bobble. Cast on 39 stitches and divide over 4 needles, putting a stitch marker at the beginning. As with the others, join into a round.

a. For round 1, knit 1 purl 1 and repeat until the end of the round.

b. For round 2, purl 1, knit 1 and repeat until the end of the round.

c. Repeat round 1 and 2 until you get to round 30.

2. Break off your yarn and leave a long tail. Thread through the darning needle. Pass through all stitches and pull tightly, weaving in the loose end and stuffing, just as you have done in previous cactus patterns.

3. Then, begin the first medium bobble. Cast on 27 stitches. Again, divide evenly over 4 double-pointed needles and put a stitch marker at the beginning of the round. Join into a round.

a. For round 1, knit 1, purl 1 and repeat until the end of the round.

b. For round 2, purl 1, knit 1 and repeat until the end of the round.

c. Repeat rounds 1 and 2 over and over until you get to 20 rounds. Then repeat step 5 with this new bobble.

4. Move on to the second medium bobble. For this one, cast on 21 stitches, divided evenly across 4 double-pointed needles

with a stitch marker and join it into a round.

    a. For round 1, knit 1 and purl 1, repeating until the end of the round.

    b. For round 2, purl 1, knit 1 and repeat until the end of the round.

    c. Repeat round 1 and 2 for 20 rounds. Then, repeat step 5 to finish this bobble.

5. Move on to the small bobble now. To complete this, cast on 15 stitches, divided evenly across 4 double-pointed needles. Put on a stitch marker and make a round.

    a. For round 1, knit 1, purl 1 until the end of the round.

    b. For round 2, purl 1, knit 1 until the end of the round.

    c. Repeat round 1 and 2 for 16 rounds.

    d. Repeat step 5 to close the cactus.

6. To attach, use a matching thread to sew the 2 medium and small bobbles onto the large where you want them. If you want to, you can add some crocheted flowers as well.

Supplies:

- 25g DK weight yarn (5 yards)
- 10g DK weight yarn in the color of your choice (1 yard)
- 3mm (US#2.5) double-pointed needles or circular needles.
- Toy Filling
- 3 buttons (safety buttons if giving to a child), beads, felt, pompoms, or embroidery threads, depending on how you want to give your snowman their face.
- Thread for smile and sewing on buttons
- Darning needle

Gauge: Irrelevant as not for wearing.

Size: 4" tall

When winter arrives, all the children dream of making snowmen and having a blast. But, if you live somewhere that snow is a bit of a rarity, you might feel like your kids are missing out. Thankfully, you now have options. You now have ways that you will be able to overcome that feeling of missing out. One way is to encourage your children to make their very own knitted snowmen instead! You can spend the time making a snowman base for your kids and leave it for them to decorate instead. All you have to do is make sure that you now have plenty of white yarn on hand, plus whatever color your children want for the scarf. Then, you're free to make this cute 'lil fellow who can help welcome the winter, even if the ground is completely snow-free. Are you ready?

As a note, in the picture, you can see that the buttons, mouth, and arms were embroidered using black. But, you can also choose to glue on pompoms or sew on buttons if you want to. Either way, you get a cute project that you can involve your kids in as well! To complete this project, you will need:

Instructions:

1. Cast on 6 stitches. Then, knit 1 row. Connect carefully to work in the round without having any stitches twist around.

    a. For round 1, knit into front and back of stitch all stitches (you now have 12 stitches).

    b. For round 2, knit into the front and back of the stitch, knit 1, and repeat until you get to the end of the round (you now have 18 stitches).

    c. For round 3, knit from front and back of the stitch, knit 2, and repeat to the end of the round. (You now have 24 stitches).

    d. For round 4, knit from front and back of the stitch, knit 3, and repeat until the end of the round (you now have 30 stitches).

    e. For round 5, knit from front and back of the stitch, knit 4, and repeat until the end of the round (you now have 36 stitches).

    f. For round 6, knit from front and back of the stitch, knit 5, and repeat until the end of the round (you now have 42 stitches).

g. For round 7, knit from front and back of the stitch, knit 6, and repeat until the end of the round (you now have 48 stitches).

h. For round 8, knit from front and back of the stitch, knit 7, and repeat until the end of the round (you now have 54 stitches).

i. For rounds 9 through 26, knit.

2. OPTIONAL: Some people like to put a bit of weight in the bottom of the pattern, adding in a small satchel of weighted beads. You can do this now, putting them in the bottom, so your snowman stays standing upright. Otherwise, continue on.

a. For round 27, knit 7, knit 2 together, and repeat until the end (you now have 48 stitches).

b. For round 28, knit 6, knit 2 together, and repeat until the end of the round (you now have 42 stitches).

c. For round 27, knit 5, knit 2 together, and repeat until the end of the round (you now have 36 stitches).

d. For round 31, knit.

e. For round 32, knit into the front and back of the stitch until the end of the round.

f. For round 33, knit into front and back of the stitch, knit 5, and repeat until the end of the round (you now have 42 stitches).

g. For round 34, knit into front and back of the stitch, knit 6, and repeat until the end of the round (you now have 48 stitches).

h. For round 35, knit into front and back of the stitch, knit 7, and repeat until the end of the round (you now have 54 stitches).

i. For rounds 36 through 49, knit.

3. Fill up the bottom half with toy stuffing, then add on any facial features that you choose to add. Then, carefully stuff its head as well. Don't worry about filling it entirely yet—you just want to get the foundation, and you can continue to add a bit of stuffing here and there until it is entirely full.

a. For round 50, knit 7, knit 2 together, and repeat until the end of the round (you now have 48 stitches).

b. For round 51, knit 6, knit 2 together, and repeat until the end of the round (you now have 42 stitches).

c. For round 52, knit 5, knit 2 together, and repeat until the end of the round (you now have 36 stitches).

d. For round 53, knit 4, knit 2 together, and repeat until the end of the round (you now have 30 stitches).

e. For round 54, knit 3, knit 2 together, and repeat until the end of the round (you now have 24 stitches).

f. For round 55, knit 2, knit 2 together, and repeat until the end of the round (you now have 18 stitches).

g. For round 56, knit 1, knit 2 together, and repeat until the end of the round (you now have 12 stitches).

h. For round 57, knit 2 together and repeat until the end of the round (you now have 6 stitches).

4. Break yarn, make sure that your head is stuffed completely and then thread it through the remaining 6 stitches so you

can sew into the end. Then, prepare to make the scarf.

a. To begin the scarf, cast on 6 stitches.

b. For row 1, slip stitch purlwise, then knit until the end of the row. Repeat each row until your scarf is long enough.

c. Then cast off and sew in the ends. Attach the scarf with a needle and thread, and add any last-minute decorations with embroidery thread. Admire your handiwork!

Chapter 2:

Intermediate and Advanced

Patterns

If you're ready for more complex patterns that will take more skill to create, then you're in the right spot. Here, provided for you are five patterns that will require more complexity to create the right way. If you want to be able to create the projects within this chapter, you will need a more nuanced skillset that will lend itself to working on your skills to ensure that they are always developing little by little.

Supplies:

- 850 yds of yarn.

- Size US 2.5 & 4 Needles

- 2.5 Circular 24" Needles

Gauge: 12-15 stitches = 4 inches

Size: 12/14 womens sweater

Who doesn't love a nice, chunky sweater sometimes? Consider this one—though time consuming, it is quite comfortable as well!

1. For the Rib, use a stocking stitch. For row one and all odd rows, knit stitches.

    a. For the second row and all even rows, purl stitches.

2. For the Back, cast on 145 stitches (count the edge stitches) on 2.5 needles. Knit rib for 1.5 inches.

3. Change needles to the Size 4 needles and knit stocking stitch for 210 rows. Cast of.

4. On the front, knit the same as the back, but the neckline is different. Cast on 145 stitches, including the edge stitches on 2.5 needles. Knit the rib for 1.5 inches. Change the needles to Size 4 needles and knit stocking stitch for 172 rows.

    a. On row 173, close 17 stitches in the middle of the front and continue knitting the left and right parts separately.

    b. For rows 175-186, close the first stitch in each odd row to shape the neckline.

c. For rows 187 through 210: Continue stocking stitch on 52 stitches. Cast off. Finish the other side the same way.

d. For the sleeve, cast on 60 stitches, including edge stitches on 2.5 needles.

5. Knit rib for 22 rows. Change needles to Size 4 needles and knit stocking stitch. Add 1 stitch on both sides of every 4th row 32 times in 128 rows. You should end with 124 stitches. Confirm, then cast off.

6. Join the shoulder seams. Pick up 80 stitches on circular needles along the neckline and knit 48 rows in rounds for the turtleneck collar. Cast off. Join the side seams and sleeve seams. Set in the sleeves, and you are done.

Supplies:

- Worsted yarn (multicolored in the picture, but you can use just one color if you prefer)

- A bit of waste yarn

- 1 set of #5 double pointed needles

Gauge: 28 sts, 40 rounds = 4 inches

Size: Adult

Need a pair of gloves to keep your hands warm? Well, you're in the right spot. If you want to be able to keep your hands cozy and toasty warm all winter long, then consider making your very own gloves. This tutorial describes the process of making a beautiful pair of women's gloves that look great and will keep you warm, too. This pattern can be altered if you wanted to use just a single color to make your glove, but this particular picture shows this glove created with a multicolored skein. Are you ready to get started?

Instructions:

Right glove

1. Cast on 30 stitches loosely with your first double-pointed needle. Then, divide the stitches evenly over four needles. You should have 7 or 8 stitches per needle. Work the cuff by making stockinette stitches as follows:

a. Using needle A, knit 1 row

b. Using needle B, knit 7 rows

c. Using needle C, knit 1 row

d. Using needle B, knit 1 row

e. Using needle C, knit 1 row

f. Using needle B, knit 1 row

g. Using needle C, knit 4 rows

h. Change to needle B. K 6, increase 1 by knitting twisted out of the horizontal thread. Knit until you're 2 stitches before the end of the row. Make 1 stitch, end by knitting 3. (you're up to 34 stitches).

i. Change to needle C. Knit 2 rows.

j. Change to needle A. Knit 1 row.

k. Change to needle C. Knit 3 rows. The glove should now be 4 inches or 33 rows long.

2. Start working on the thumb stitches now. Go back to needle A. Knit 1. Using waste yarn, knit 6, then slip the 6 stitches back to the left needle and knit them again with A. Knit through the whole row.

3. Change to C and knit 8 rows.

4. Start working on the pinkie finger.

   a. Work up to within 4 stitches of the end of the second needle.

   b. Work the 4 stitches, then the first four stitches on the third needle, and cast on 2 stitches, having them come from the back of the glove toward the palm.

   c. Divide the 10 stitches among 3 needles, working in the round for 18 rounds.

   d. Knit 2 together 5 times, then cut the yarn and draw the 5 stitches together with the yarn.

   e. Begin with a new piece of yarn. Knit 2 from the fourchette, then work 1 round over the stitches to the ring finger.

5. Begin the ring finger.

   a. Work to within 4 stitches before the end of the second needle. Knit the 4 stitches, the 2 stitches of the fourchette, and the first 4 stitches on the third needle, then cast on 2 stitches to serve as the next fourchette.

b. Divide these 12 into 3 needles. Work in the round for 22 rounds, or for 2.7 inches.

c. Knit 2 together and repeat 6 times.

d. Cut the yarn and draw the six stitches together.

6. For the middle finger, put the first 5 stitches onto your first needle and the last 5 on the fourth needle using waste yarn for the forefinger.

a. Begin from the backside, using a new piece of yarn. Knit 4. Then, nit 2 form the fourchette.

b. Knit 4, then cast on 2 stitches to become the next fourchette.

c. Divide the 12 stitches among 3 needles and work in the round for 24 rounds.

d. Knit 2 together 6 times, then cut the yarn and draw the 6 stitches together with the yarn.

7. Begin working on the forefinger.

a. Knit 2 from the fourchette.

b. Then, knit 10 from the waste yarn. Divide into 12 stitches among 3 needles.

   c. Work in the round for 22 rounds.

   d. Knit 2 together 6 times, then cut the yarn and draw the 6 stitches together with yarn.

8. Finish the thumb.

   a. Using a new piece of yarn, knit 6 from the waste yarn.

   b. Make 1, knit 6, make 1.

   c. Then, divide these 14 stitches among 3 needles. Work in the round for 18 rounds.

   d. Knit 2 together 7 times. Cut the yarn and draw the 7 stitches together using yarn.

Left glove

1. To make the left glove, you really need to know how to change the position of the thumb. Everything else will be worked the same way. Cast 30 stitches with needle A. Divide among 4 needles. Work in the stockinette stitch for the following:

   a. A: Knit 1 row

   b. B: Knit 7 rows

   c. C: Knit 1 row

d. B Knit 1 row

e. C: Knit 1 row

f. B Knit 1 row

g. C Knit 4 rows

h. Change to B. Knit 2, make 1, knit to within 6 stitches of the end of your row. Make 1 and end with knit 6 (you have 32 stitches total).

i. Change to C. Knit 2 rows.

j. Change to A. Knit 1 row.

k. Change to C. Knit 3 rows.

l. Change to A. Knit 4 rows. In that fourth row, knit 3, make 1, knit to within 7 stitches of the end, make 1, knit 7 (you have 34 stitches total).

m. Change to C. Knit 2 rows.

n. Change to A. Knit 1 row.

o. Change to C. Knit 3 rows.

2. Then, change to A to create the thumb stitches. Knit to within 7 stitches of the end of the row. Using waste yarn, knit 6. Slip the 6 stitches back to the left needle and repeat the knitting with A. End knitting 1.

3. Change to C. Knit 8 rows.

4. Follow the instructions for the right hand for the rest of the fingers.

5. To finish, weave in the ends. Block if desired.

Supplies:

- 30 yards of multi-colored fingering weight yarn

- A 2.5mm or 3mm crochet hook

- Long 3.5mm circular needles

- Scrap yarn to use for a provisional cast on

- Tapestry needle

Gauge: 28 sts, 40 rounds = 4 inches

Size: Adult

If you want to keep your hands warm once the weather cools while also wearing something your friends do not have, try this pattern out. You will be left with warm, fingerless mitts with a neat serpentine pattern that you can customize to your heart's content. Make these as understated or as loud as you wish.

Instructions:

1. Provisionally crochet on 45 stitches, which means you crochet on stitches with the scrap yarn and knit your first row with the yarn you intend to use for the full project.

2. Use this pattern using stockinette stitch:

   a. Row 1-Right Side: Slip 1, knit to the end of the row

   b. Row 2-Wrong Side: Slip 1, purl to the end of the row

   c. Repeat until you have 11 rows of stockinette stitch.

   d. For row 12, add random loops and curves of surface crochet on the right side. Make sure to cross the complete width of the mitt, finishing near the end of the row. The needle tip should be on the opposite side of your yarn, so slip all stitches and add the last crochet loop to the knitting needle.

   e. For row 13 on the Right Side, slip 2, pass the first slipped stitch over the second slipped stitch, knit 9, place a marker, and knit to the end.

3. Row 14 (Wrong Side, this is the thumb row: Slip 1, purl to last stitch before marker, knit 1, turn, but do not wrap the yarn around the next stitch (as you want an opening for the thumb)

   a. knit 12, wrap and turn, knit 11, purl 1, turn (do not wrap here or at the end of the next lines of instruction)

   b. Knit 11, wrap and turn, purl 10, knit 1, turn

   c. Knit 9, wrap and turn, purl 8, knit 1, turn

   d. Knit 7, wrap and turn, purl 6, knit 1, turn

   e. Knit 6, wrap and turn, purl 5, knit 1, turn

   f. Knit 4, wrap and turn, purl 3, knit 1, turn

   g. Knit 5, wrap and turn, purl 4, knit 1, turn

   h. Knit 9, wrap and turn, purl 8, knit 1, turn

   i. Purl until the end.

4. Row 15 on the Right Side: slip 1, knit to the end.

5. Row 16 on the Wrong Side: Slip 1, purl to the end.

   a. Make four more rows of stockinette stitch.

6. For row 20 on the Wrong Side, slip 1, purl 39, wrap and turn, knit 20, wrap and turn, purl to the end of the row.

   a. Knit four more rows of stockinette stitch. Then, on row 24, apply surface crochet using the same method as row 12.

7. Row 25 on the Right side: slip 1, knit to the end.

8. Row 26, slip 1, purl to the end. Knit in stockinette through row 29.

9. Row 30 on the Wrong Side: Slip 1, purl 39, wrap and turn, knit 20, wrap and turn, purl to the end.

10. Row 31, slip1, knit to the end.

11. Row 32, add surface crochet just like before.

   a. Repeat the pattern for rows 25 through 32 two more times, or as needed until to fit your hands. Then do five more rows of stockinette stitch.

12. Remove the provisional cast on and place the stitches on a second needle.

13. Graft on stockinette stitch with the tapestry needle and get started on the second mitt.

14. Follow the same pattern up until the thumb row described earlier. Instead, have row 14 just be a normal purl, then start your next row as follows:

    a. Slip 1, knit to the last stitch before your marker, purl 1, turn

    b. Purl 12, wrap and turn, knit 11, purl 1, turn

    c. Purl 11, wrap and turn, knit 10, purl 1, turn

    d. Purl 9, wrap and turn, knit 8, purl 1, turn

    e. Purl 7, wrap and turn, knit 6, purl 1, turn

    f. Purl 6, wrap and turn, knit 5, purl 1, turn

    g. Purl 4, wrap and turn, knit 4, purl 1, turn

    h. Purl 9, wrap and turn, knit 8, purl 1, turn

    i. Knit to the end.

15. From here, continue the pattern as normal, moving the shaping row up 1, replacing the original row with normal purling. When doing the shaping row, slip 1, knit 39, wrap and turn, purl 20, wrap and turn, knit to the end.

Supplies:

- Three buttons
- 568 yards of yarn
- Cable needle
- Stitch holders
- Stitch markers

- Tapestry needle

- US Size 4 24" circular double-pointed knitting needles

- US Size 6 24" circular knitting needles

Gauge: 20 sts x 36 rows = 4"

Size: 2T toddler

If you are looking for a cute accessory to give your young child, make them a cardigan. This base pattern is for a 2T sized cardigan. Adjust to get the right fit for your young one.

Instructions:

1. For the body, cast on 114 stitches on the larger needles. For the first row, do the following:

   a) On the Right Side, knit 26 stitches for the left front, place marker for the side, knit 62 stitches for the pack, place marker for the side, knit 26 stitches for the Right Front.

   b) On the next row on the wrong side, purl 1, knit to the last stitch, purl 1. Do eight more rows in garter stitch, keeping the first stitch on each edge in stockinette.

2. To set up the pattern, do the following in the next row

   a) Knit 4, place marker, purl 1, right twist, purl 2, knit 1, make 1, knit 1, purl 2, knit 1, make 1, knit 1, purl 2, right twist, purl 1, place a marker

   b) Knit to side marker, slip marker, knit 6, place marker

   c) Work to place marker knit 18, place marker, work to place marker, knit to side marker, slip marker, knit 6, place marker, work to place marker, knit to end. 8 stitches should be increased to 122 stitches.

3. For the following row, purl 1, knit to marker.

   a) work Row 2 of 4x4 Right Cross Chart over 18 stitches to marker, knit to side marker, slip marker, knit to marker, work Row 2 of 4x4

   b) Left Cross Chart over 18 stitches to marker, knit to marker, work Row 2 of 4x4 Right Cross Chart over 18 stitches to marker, knit to side marker.

   c) slip marker, knit to marker, work row 2 of 4x4 Left Cross Chart over 18 stitches to marker, knit to last stitch, purl 1.

d) Continue the pattern, keeping stitches outside markers in garter stitch with 1 edge stitch in stockinette stitch through row 26 of Charts.

e) Repeat Rows 9-26 of Charts. Work even in pattern until the body measures 6 inches from cast-on edge, ending on a Wrong Side row.

4. For the neck, you need to make a decrease row.

a) Starting on the Right Side: Knit 2 together, work in this pattern to the last 2 stitches- slip, slip, knit, 2 stitches decreased.

b) Repeat the decrease row every 14 rows three more times. The neck shaping will continue through the remainder of the project. When the body measures 7", cast-on edge, end with a Wrong Side row, and proceed.

5. To separate the back and front, work this pattern:

a) Across Right Front stitches to 2 stitches before side marker, bind off next 4 stitches.

b) Work in this pattern across the back stitches to 2 stitches before side marker, bind off the next 4 stitches.

c) Work in pattern across Left Front stitches. Place Right front stitches on holder along with back stitches.

6. For the Left Front, work a wrong side row to make the pattern even. Decrease on the Right side by doing the following:

a) Knit 1, knit 2 together, work in pattern to the end.

b) The first decrease will happen at the armhole edge. Repeat the decrease row on the Right Side row one more time.

c) Work the pattern evenly until the armhole measures 4.5 inches. End with a Wrong Side row.

d) When the armhole and neck decrease is done, you should have 20 stitches left for the Shoulder.

e) Bind off all stitches.

7. For the Right Front, return the stitches to the needle and work a Wrong Side row to even out the pattern.

8. Start a decrease row on the Right Side by doing the following:

   a) Work the pattern to the last 3 stitches, slip, slip, knit, knit 1.

   b) The first decrease should be at the armhole edge. Repeat this row one more time. Work the pattern evenly until the Armhole measures 4.5 inches. End on a Wrong Side Row. When the armhole and neck decreases are done, 20 stitches remain for the Shoulder. Bind off all stitches.

9. For the back, return the stitches to the needle. Work a Wrong Side row to even out your pattern.

10. Begin a decrease by doing the following: Knit 1, knit 2 together.

    a) Work in this pattern to the last 3 stitches, then slip, slip, knit, knit 1 stitch.

    b) Repeat this row once more. 58 stitches should remain. Work evenly in the pattern until the armhole measures 4.5 inches, end on a Wrong Side row.

11. For the Right Sleeve, cast on 30 stitches.

    a) For row 1 on the Right Side, knit.

    b) On row 2, purl 1, knit to the last stitch, purl 1.

    c) Repeat these two rows 4 more times.

12. For the Main Sleeve, set up your first row as follows:

    a) Knit 7 stitches, place marker, purl 1, right twist, purl 2, knit 1, make 1, knit 1, purl 2, knit 1, make 1, knit 1, purl 2, right twist, purl 1, place marker, knit to the end.

    b) You should have 2 stitches increased, with a total of 32.

13. On the Wrong Side, Purl 1, knit to marker, slip marker, work row 2 of Right Cross Chart to marker, slip marker, knit to the last stitch, purl 1.

    a) Continue this pattern for 2 more rows.

14. Now make an increase row by doing the following:

a) Knit 1, make 1, work in this pattern to the last stitch, make 1, knit 1. Repeat increase row every 6 rows, five more times. You should have 42 stitches. Work evenly in the pattern until the Sleeve measures 7 inches from cast-on edge and end in a Wrong Side row.

15. For the Shape Cap, bind off 2 stitches at the beginning of the next 2 rows. You should have 38 stitches remaining.

16. Decrease by doing the following: knit 1, knit 2 together, working in this pattern to the last 2 stitches, then slip, slip, knit, knit 1. 2 stitches should be decreased.

a) Repeat the decrease row every 3 Right Side rows 4 more times, every 2 Right side rows 0 times, and every Right side Row 1 time, leaving you with 26 stitches.

b) Bind off 4 stitches at the beginning of the next 4 rows. Bind off the remaining 10 stitches.

17. For the left sleeve, work the same as the Right Sleeve, substituting the Left Cross chart for the Right Cross chart.

18. Sew the Should seams. Sew the Sleeve Caps into the armholes. Sew the Sleeve and Side Seams.

19. For the Shawl Collar, with the smaller needle, begin at the lower Right Front edge, knit 32 stitches to the beginning of Neck Shaping.

   a) Place marker 32 stitches up the remainder of Right Front, 18 stitches along with Back Neck, 32 stitches down Left Front to the beginning of Neck Shaping.

   b) Place marker, 32 stitches down left front Edge. You should have 146 stitches. Knit a Wrong Side row.

20. To shape the Collar, do the following:

   a) Row 1 should be the Right Side-Knit to the first stitch before the second marker, wrap next stitch and turn.

   b) Knit to the first stitch before the first marker, wrap next stitch, and turn.

   c) Knit to 2 stitches before last wrapped stitch, wrap next stitch, and turn.

   d) Knit to 2 stitches before last wrapped stitch, wrap next stitch, and turn.

e) Repeat the last 2 rows 2 more times with 4 wrapped stitches at each end.

f) Knit to 3 stitches before last wrapped stitch, wrap next stitch, and turn.

g) Knit to 3 stitches before last wrapped stitch, wrap next stitch, and turn.

h) Repeat the last 2 rows 7 more times, 12 wrapped stitches each end.

i) Knit to end in this row and the next.

j) Continue in garter stitch until Collar measures 1.25 inches, and end with a Right Side row.

21. For the Buttonhole Row, start on the Wrong Side and knit 6,

a) Knit 2 together, yarn over, knit 8 stitches. Repeat this process until you get to 2 stitches before marker, knit 2 together, yarn over, knit to the end.

b) You should have three buttonholes.

c) Continue in garter stitch until collar measures 1.75 inches, and end on a Wrong Side Row.

22. For the bind off, cast on 3 stitches to the first stitch on the left needle, * (knit 2,

knit 2 together through the back loop, slip these 3 stitches back to left needle).

a) Do the steps in parentheses 5 times. Knit 2, knit 3 together through the back loop, slip these stitches back to the left needle.

b) Repeat from the * until all stitches from Collar have been bound off. 3 stitches remain, slip 1, knit 2 together, pass slip stitch over, fasten off the last stitch.

23. Weave in the ends. Block the sweater and so in the buttons to the Right Front, opposite the buttonholes.

Supplies:

- Thick wool (250 yds)

- 3.5mm needles

- Cable needle

- Darning needle

- Stitch markers

- Tape measure

Gauge: 32 sts x 32 rows = 4"

Size: Small adult

Sometimes, you want a hat that is going to provide a bit more texture to your outfit, and when that's the case, you can't go wrong with this cabled hat! This pattern is a bit more complex than the options that you've seen thus far, but it is great if you want to learn how to master your skills and push yourself further. To create this project, you will need:

Instructions:

1. Cast off 96 stitches.

    a. Place your round marker and join into the round.

    b. Work 2x2 ribbing (knit 2, purl 2) until the end of the row for 1.5 inches of a hat or until the brim is the right size. Switch to larger needles.

    c. Increase the next round, going knit 12, make 1, until you get to the end. You should add 8 stitches, bringing your total up to 104.

    d. Begin cabled ribbing. Rounds 1-7 should be knit 1 through the back loop, purl 1 to end.

    e. Round 8 should be slip 3 stitches to cable needle and hold at front. Purl 1. Repeat until the end of the round.

    f. Repeat the previous 8 rounds 3 times until you have a total of 7 inches.

    g. Go around once more, marking every 13 stitches.

2. Begin decreasing crown.

    a. Round 1, work in pattern to 2 stitches before the marker. Slip, slip, knit.

    b. Slip marker. Repeat until the end of the round, decreasing 8 stitches.

    c. Round 2, work around in the same pattern.

    d. Repeat steps 8 and 9 until you have just 40 stitches remaining.

    e. Work 2 more rounds, going slip, slip knit until end, decreasing to 10 stitches left.

3. To finish, break the yarn and leave a 6-inch tail. With a tapestry needle, weave the tail into the remaining stitches and pull tightly to cinch it closed. Then, if you want to, add a pompom.

Conclusion

Thank you for going through these various patterns that have been provided to you. Hopefully, as you read through these, you've found yourself discovering how better to work on your own knitting skills. Remember, the best way to improve is to practice! Have fun out there, and don't forget to check back for more knitting patterns in the future!

If you've found that these patterns are fun or easy to enjoy, please consider leaving a review on Amazon with your experience! It'd be great to hear from you.

Exclusive 5-day bonus course just for you!

We will be sharing top crafting mistakes to avoid, how to save money on supplies and extra craft patterns!

Simply let us know where to send the course e-mails to via this link below.

https://bit.ly/nancy-gordon

For any general feedback & enquiries, you can reach us at bookgrowthpublishing@mail.com

Credits

Easy Baby Booties Pattern Image, pg. 5: "Baby Booties" by Sarah&Boston is licensed under CC BY-SA 2.0

Baby Bibs Pattern Image, pg. 7: "baby bib" by moonrat42 is licensed under CC BY-SA 2.0

Easy Knit Shawl Pattern Image, pg. 11: "Prairie House Heather Shawl" by starathena is licensed under CC BY 2.0

Bunny Eared Hat Pattern Image, pg. 13: "Bunny Hat" by anniehp is licensed under CC BY 2.0

Knitted Cat Toys Image, pg. 19: "Mindy Mouse" by Wednesday Elf - Mountainside Crochet is licensed under CC BY 2.0

Knitted Hedgehog Pattern Image, pg. 26: "Amigurumi Hedehog" by toadstool ring is licensed under CC BY 2.0

Coasters Pattern Image, pg. 29: "knit coaster" by zappowbang is licensed under CC BY 2.0

Printed in Great Britain
by Amazon